D1399341

This Planner Belongs To :

_____

Copyright 2018

All rights reserved. No part of this publication may be reproduced, stored in a retrieval system, or transmitted in any form
or by any means, electronic, mechanical, photocopying, recording or otherwise, without the prior written permission of the publisher.

Printed by CreateSpace, An Amazon.com Company
A Publication by Jada Correia

Success Doesn't

Just Happen

It's Planned For.

Monthly Budget

Income		
Income 1		
Income 2		
Other Income		
TOTAL INCOME		

Expenses

Month :

Budget :

Bill To Be Paid	Date Due	Amount	Paid	Note
			○	
			○	
			○	
			○	
			○	
			○	
			○	
			○	
			○	
			○	
			○	
			○	
			○	
			○	
			○	
			○	
			○	
			○	
			○	
			○	
TOTAL				

Monthly Budget

Other Expenses	Date	Amount	Note
TOTAL			

TOTAL INCOME

TOTAL EXPENSES

DIFFERENCE

Notes

Weekly Expense Tracker

Month : _____   Week Of : _____   Budget : _____

Monday   Date ....../....../......

Description	Amount
Total	

Tuesday   Date ....../....../......

Description	Amount
Total	

Wednesday   Date ....../....../......

Description	Amount
Total	

Thursday   Date ....../....../......

Description	Amount
Total	

Weekly Expense Tracker

Total Expenses :

Balance :

Friday

Date ..../......./.......

Description	Amount
Total	

Saturday

Date ..../......./.......

Description	Amount
Total	

Sunday

Date ..../......./.......

Description	Amount
Total	

Notes

Weekly Expense Tracker

Month :   **Week Of :**   **Budget :**

Monday   Date ..../......./.......

Description	Amount
Total	

Tuesday   Date ..../......./.......

Description	Amount
Total	

Wednesday   Date ..../......./.......

Description	Amount
Total	

Thursday   Date ..../......./.......

Description	Amount
Total	

Weekly Expense Tracker

Total Expenses :   **Balance :**

Friday   Date ….../….../…....

Description	Amount
Total	

Saturday   Date ….../….../…....

Description	Amount
Total	

Sunday   Date ….../….../…....

Description	Amount
Total	

Notes

_____

_____

_____

_____

_____

_____

_____

_____

_____

_____

Weekly Expense Tracker

Month : _____   Week Of : _____   Budget : _____

Monday   Date ....../....../......

Description	Amount
Total	

Tuesday   Date ....../....../......

Description	Amount
Total	

Wednesday   Date ....../....../......

Description	Amount
Total	

Thursday   Date ....../....../......

Description	Amount
Total	

Weekly Expense Tracker

Total Expenses :   **Balance :**

Friday   Date ..../......./.......

Description	Amount
Total	

Saturday   Date ..../......./.......

Description	Amount
Total	

Sunday   Date ..../......./.......

Description	Amount
Total	

Notes

_____

_____

_____

_____

_____

_____

_____

_____

_____

_____

Weekly Expense Tracker

Month : _____   **Week Of :** _____   **Budget :** _____

Monday   Date ..../......./.......

Description	Amount
Total	

Tuesday   Date ..../......./.......

Description	Amount
Total	

Wednesday   Date ..../......./.......

Description	Amount
Total	

Thursday   Date ..../......./.......

Description	Amount
Total	

Weekly Expense Tracker

Total Expenses : _____   **Balance :** _____

Friday   Date ..../......./.......

Description	Amount
Total	

Saturday   Date ..../......./.......

Description	Amount
Total	

Sunday   Date ..../......./.......

Description	Amount
Total	

Notes

_____

_____

_____

_____

_____

_____

_____

_____

_____

_____

_____

Weekly Expense Tracker

Month : _____   Week Of : _____   Budget : _____

Monday   Date ..../......./.......

Description	Amount
Total	

Tuesday   Date ..../......./.......

Description	Amount
Total	

Wednesday   Date ..../......./.......

Description	Amount
Total	

Thursday   Date ..../......./.......

Description	Amount
Total	

Weekly Expense Tracker

Total Expenses :

Balance :

Friday

Date ....../....../......

Description	Amount
Total	

Saturday

Date ....../....../......

Description	Amount
Total	

Sunday

Date ....../....../......

Description	Amount
Total	

Notes

Monthly Budget

Income		
Income 1		
Income 2		
Other Income		
TOTAL INCOME		

Expenses

Month :

Budget :

Bill To Be Paid	Date Due	Amount	Paid	Note
			○	
			○	
			○	
			○	
			○	
			○	
			○	
			○	
			○	
			○	
			○	
			○	
			○	
			○	
			○	
			○	
			○	
			○	
			○	
TOTAL				

Monthly Budget

Other Expenses	Date	Amount	Note
TOTAL			

TOTAL INCOME

TOTAL EXPENSES

DIFFERENCE

Notes

Weekly Expense Tracker

Month : **Week Of :** **Budget :**

Monday
Date ..../......./.......

Description	Amount
Total	

Tuesday
Date ..../......./.......

Description	Amount
Total	

Wednesday
Date ..../......./.......

Description	Amount
Total	

Thursday
Date ..../......./.......

Description	Amount
Total	

Weekly Expense Tracker

Total Expenses :   **Balance :**

Friday   Date ..../......./.......

Description	Amount
Total	

Saturday   Date ..../......./.......

Description	Amount
Total	

Sunday   Date ..../......./.......

Description	Amount
Total	

Notes

Weekly Expense Tracker

Month : _____   Week Of : _____   Budget : _____

Monday   Date ..../......./.......

Description	Amount
Total	

Tuesday   Date ..../......./.......

Description	Amount
Total	

Wednesday   Date ..../......./.......

Description	Amount
Total	

Thursday   Date ..../......./.......

Description	Amount
Total	

Weekly Expense Tracker

Total Expenses :   **Balance :**

Friday   Date ....../....../......

Description	Amount
Total	

Saturday   Date ....../....../......

Description	Amount
Total	

Sunday   Date ....../....../......

Description	Amount
Total	

Notes

Weekly Expense Tracker

Month : _____ **Week Of :** _____ **Budget :** _____

Monday
Date ..../......./.......

Description	Amount
Total	

Tuesday
Date ..../......./.......

Description	Amount
Total	

Wednesday
Date ..../......./.......

Description	Amount
Total	

Thursday
Date ..../......./.......

Description	Amount
Total	

Weekly Expense Tracker

Total Expenses :   **Balance :**

Friday   Date ..../......./.......

Description	Amount
Total	

Saturday   Date ..../......./.......

Description	Amount
Total	

Sunday   Date ..../......./.......

Description	Amount
Total	

Notes

_____
_____
_____
_____
_____
_____
_____
_____
_____
_____
_____

Weekly Expense Tracker

Month : _____ **Week Of :** _____ **Budget :** _____

Monday
Date ..../......../........

Description	Amount
Total	

Tuesday
Date ..../......../........

Description	Amount
Total	

Wednesday
Date ..../......../........

Description	Amount
Total	

Thursday
Date ..../......../........

Description	Amount
Total	

Weekly Expense Tracker

Total Expenses :

Balance :

Friday
Date ..../......./.......

Description	Amount
Total	

Saturday
Date ..../......./.......

Description	Amount
Total	

Sunday
Date ..../......./.......

Description	Amount
Total	

Notes

Weekly Expense Tracker

Month : _____   Week Of : _____   Budget : _____

Monday
Date ....../....../......

Description	Amount
Total	

Tuesday
Date ....../....../......

Description	Amount
Total	

Wednesday
Date ....../....../......

Description	Amount
Total	

Thursday
Date ....../....../......

Description	Amount
Total	

Weekly Expense Tracker

Total Expenses :   **Balance :**

Friday   Date ..../......./.......

Description	Amount
Total	

Saturday   Date ..../......./.......

Description	Amount
Total	

Sunday   Date ..../......./.......

Description	Amount
Total	

Notes

Monthly Budget

Income		
Income 1		
Income 2		
Other Income		
TOTAL INCOME		

Expenses

Month :

Budget :

Bill To Be Paid	Date Due	Amount	Paid	Note
			○	
			○	
			○	
			○	
			○	
			○	
			○	
			○	
			○	
			○	
			○	
			○	
			○	
			○	
			○	
			○	
			○	
			○	
			○	
TOTAL				

Monthly Budget

Other Expenses	Date	Amount	Note
TOTAL			

TOTAL INCOME

TOTAL EXPENSES

DIFFERENCE

Notes

Weekly Expense Tracker

Month : _____   Week Of : _____   Budget : _____

Monday   Date ..../......./.......

Description	Amount
Total	

Tuesday   Date ..../......./.......

Description	Amount
Total	

Wednesday   Date ..../......./.......

Description	Amount
Total	

Thursday   Date ..../......./.......

Description	Amount
Total	

Weekly Expense Tracker

Total Expenses : _____ **Balance :** _____

Friday

Date ..../......./.......

Description	Amount
Total	

Saturday

Date ..../......./.......

Description	Amount
Total	

Sunday

Date ..../......./.......

Description	Amount
Total	

Notes

_____
_____
_____
_____
_____
_____
_____
_____
_____
_____
_____

Weekly Expense Tracker

Month : _____   Week Of : _____   Budget : _____

Monday
Date ..../......./.......

Description	Amount
Total	

Tuesday
Date ..../......./.......

Description	Amount
Total	

Wednesday
Date ..../......./.......

Description	Amount
Total	

Thursday
Date ..../......./.......

Description	Amount
Total	

Weekly Expense Tracker

Total Expenses :   **Balance :**

Friday   Date ..../......./.......

Description	Amount
Total	

Saturday   Date ..../......./.......

Description	Amount
Total	

Sunday   Date ..../......./.......

Description	Amount
Total	

Notes

Weekly Expense Tracker

Month : _____   Week Of : _____   Budget : _____

Monday   Date ..../......./.......

Description	Amount
Total	

Tuesday   Date ..../......./.......

Description	Amount
Total	

Wednesday   Date ..../......./.......

Description	Amount
Total	

Thursday   Date ..../......./.......

Description	Amount
Total	

Weekly Expense Tracker

Total Expenses :   **Balance :**

Friday   Date ..../......./.......

Description	Amount
Total	

Saturday   Date ..../......./.......

Description	Amount
Total	

Sunday   Date ..../......./.......

Description	Amount
Total	

Notes

_____
_____
_____
_____
_____
_____
_____
_____
_____
_____

Weekly Expense Tracker

Month :   **Week Of :**   **Budget :**

Monday   Date ..../......./.......

Description	Amount
Total	

Tuesday   Date ..../......./.......

Description	Amount
Total	

Wednesday   Date ..../......./.......

Description	Amount
Total	

Thursday   Date ..../......./.......

Description	Amount
Total	

Weekly Expense Tracker

Total Expenses :   **Balance :**

Friday   Date ....../....../......

Description	Amount
Total	

Saturday   Date ....../....../......

Description	Amount
Total	

Sunday   Date ....../....../......

Description	Amount
Total	

Notes

Weekly Expense Tracker

Month : _____   Week Of : _____   Budget : _____

Monday   Date ..../......./.......

Description	Amount
Total	

Tuesday   Date ..../......./.......

Description	Amount
Total	

Wednesday   Date ..../......./.......

Description	Amount
Total	

Thursday   Date ..../......./.......

Description	Amount
Total	

Weekly Expense Tracker

Total Expenses :   **Balance :**

Friday   Date ....../....../......

Description	Amount
Total	

Saturday   Date ....../....../......

Description	Amount
Total	

Sunday   Date ....../....../......

Description	Amount
Total	

Notes

Monthly Budget

Income		
Income 1		
Income 2		
Other Income		
TOTAL INCOME		

Expenses

Month :

Budget :

Bill To Be Paid	Date Due	Amount	Paid	Note
			◯	
			◯	
			◯	
			◯	
			◯	
			◯	
			◯	
			◯	
			◯	
			◯	
			◯	
			◯	
			◯	
			◯	
			◯	
			◯	
			◯	
			◯	
			◯	
TOTAL				

Monthly Budget

Other Expenses	Date	Amount	Note
TOTAL			

TOTAL INCOME

TOTAL EXPENSES

DIFFERENCE

Notes

Weekly Expense Tracker

Month :   **Week Of :**   **Budget :**

Monday   Date ..../......./.......

Description	Amount
Total	

Tuesday   Date ..../......./.......

Description	Amount
Total	

Wednesday   Date ..../......./.......

Description	Amount
Total	

Thursday   Date ..../......./.......

Description	Amount
Total	

Weekly Expense Tracker

Total Expenses :

Balance :

Friday

Date ..../......./.......

Description	Amount
Total	

Saturday

Date ..../......./.......

Description	Amount
Total	

Sunday

Date ..../......./.......

Description	Amount
Total	

Notes

Weekly Expense Tracker

Month :   **Week Of :**   **Budget :**

Monday
Date ..../......./.......

Description	Amount
Total	

Tuesday
Date ..../......./.......

Description	Amount
Total	

Wednesday
Date ..../......./.......

Description	Amount
Total	

Thursday
Date ..../......./.......

Description	Amount
Total	

Weekly Expense Tracker

Total Expenses :   **Balance :**

Friday   Date ....../....../......

Description	Amount
Total	

Saturday   Date ....../....../......

Description	Amount
Total	

Sunday   Date ....../....../......

Description	Amount
Total	

Notes

Weekly Expense Tracker

Month : **Week Of :** **Budget :**

Monday   Date ....../....../......

Description	Amount
Total	

Tuesday   Date ....../....../......

Description	Amount
Total	

Wednesday   Date ....../....../......

Description	Amount
Total	

Thursday   Date ....../....../......

Description	Amount
Total	

Weekly Expense Tracker

Total Expenses :   **Balance :**

Friday   Date ....../....../......

Description	Amount
Total	

Saturday   Date ....../....../......

Description	Amount
Total	

Sunday   Date ....../....../......

Description	Amount
Total	

Notes

Weekly Expense Tracker

Month :   **Week Of :**   **Budget :**

Monday   Date ..../......./.......

Description	Amount
Total	

Tuesday   Date ..../......./.......

Description	Amount
Total	

Wednesday   Date ..../......./.......

Description	Amount
Total	

Thursday   Date ..../......./.......

Description	Amount
Total	

Weekly Expense Tracker

Total Expenses :

Balance :

Friday
Date ..../......./.......

Description	Amount
Total	

Saturday
Date ..../......./.......

Description	Amount
Total	

Sunday
Date ..../......./.......

Description	Amount
Total	

Notes

Weekly Expense Tracker

Month : _____ **Week Of :** _____ **Budget :** _____

Monday   Date ....../....../......

Description	Amount
Total	

Tuesday   Date ....../....../......

Description	Amount
Total	

Wednesday   Date ....../....../......

Description	Amount
Total	

Thursday   Date ....../....../......

Description	Amount
Total	

Weekly Expense Tracker

Total Expenses :   **Balance :**

Friday   Date ....../....../......

Description	Amount
Total	

Saturday   Date ....../....../......

Description	Amount
Total	

Sunday   Date ....../....../......

Description	Amount
Total	

Notes

Monthly Budget

Income		
Income 1		
Income 2		
Other Income		
TOTAL INCOME		

Expenses

Month :

Budget :

Bill To Be Paid	Date Due	Amount	Paid	Note
			◯	
			◯	
			◯	
			◯	
			◯	
			◯	
			◯	
			◯	
			◯	
			◯	
			◯	
			◯	
			◯	
			◯	
			◯	
			◯	
			◯	
			◯	
TOTAL				

Monthly Budget

Other Expenses	Date	Amount	Note
TOTAL			

TOTAL INCOME

TOTAL EXPENSES

DIFFERENCE

Notes

Weekly Expense Tracker

Month : _____ **Week Of :** _____ **Budget :** _____

Monday Date ..../......./.......

Description	Amount
Total	

Tuesday Date ..../......./.......

Description	Amount
Total	

Wednesday Date ..../......./.......

Description	Amount
Total	

Thursday Date ..../......./.......

Description	Amount
Total	

Weekly Expense Tracker

Total Expenses :

Balance :

Friday

Date ..../......./.......

Description	Amount
Total	

Saturday

Date ..../......./.......

Description	Amount
Total	

Sunday

Date ..../......./.......

Description	Amount
Total	

Notes

Weekly Expense Tracker

Month : _____ **Week Of :** _____ **Budget :** _____

Monday Date ..../......./.......

Description	Amount
Total	

Tuesday Date ..../......./.......

Description	Amount
Total	

Wednesday Date ..../......./.......

Description	Amount
Total	

Thursday Date ..../......./.......

Description	Amount
Total	

Weekly Expense Tracker

Total Expenses : **Balance :**

Friday Date ..../......./.......

Description	Amount
Total	

Saturday Date ..../......./.......

Description	Amount
Total	

Sunday Date ..../......./.......

Description	Amount
Total	

Notes

Weekly Expense Tracker

Month : _____   Week Of : _____   Budget : _____

Monday   Date ..../......../........

Description	Amount
Total	

Tuesday   Date ..../......../........

Description	Amount
Total	

Wednesday   Date ..../......../........

Description	Amount
Total	

Thursday   Date ..../......../........

Description	Amount
Total	

Weekly Expense Tracker

Total Expenses :

Balance :

Friday
Date ..../......./.......

Description	Amount
Total	

Saturday
Date ..../......./.......

Description	Amount
Total	

Sunday
Date ..../......./.......

Description	Amount
Total	

Notes
_____
_____
_____
_____
_____
_____
_____
_____
_____
_____

Weekly Expense Tracker

Month : _____   Week Of : _____   Budget : _____

Monday
Date ....../....../......

Description	Amount
Total	

Tuesday
Date ....../....../......

Description	Amount
Total	

Wednesday
Date ....../....../......

Description	Amount
Total	

Thursday
Date ....../....../......

Description	Amount
Total	

Weekly Expense Tracker

Total Expenses :　　　　　　　　　　　　　　**Balance :**

Friday　　Date ..../......./.......

Description	Amount
Total	

Saturday　　Date ..../......./.......

Description	Amount
Total	

Sunday　　Date ..../......./.......

Description	Amount
Total	

Notes

Weekly Expense Tracker

Month :   **Week Of :**   **Budget :**

Monday   Date ..../......./.......

Description	Amount
Total	

Tuesday   Date ..../......./.......

Description	Amount
Total	

Wednesday   Date ..../......./.......

Description	Amount
Total	

Thursday   Date ..../......./.......

Description	Amount
Total	

Weekly Expense Tracker

Total Expenses :   Balance :

Friday
Date ..../......./.......

Description	Amount
Total	

Saturday
Date ..../......./.......

Description	Amount
Total	

Sunday
Date ..../......./.......

Description	Amount
Total	

Notes

_____
_____
_____
_____
_____
_____
_____
_____
_____
_____
_____

Monthly Budget

Income

Income	
Income 1	
Income 2	
Other Income	
TOTAL INCOME	

Expenses

Month :

Budget :

Bill To Be Paid	Date Due	Amount	Paid	Note
			◯	
			◯	
			◯	
			◯	
			◯	
			◯	
			◯	
			◯	
			◯	
			◯	
			◯	
			◯	
			◯	
			◯	
			◯	
			◯	
			◯	
			◯	
			◯	
TOTAL				

Monthly Budget

Other Expenses	Date	Amount	Note
TOTAL			

TOTAL INCOME

TOTAL EXPENSES

DIFFERENCE

Notes

Weekly Expense Tracker

Month : **Week Of :** **Budget :**

Monday
Date ..../......./.......

Description	Amount
Total	

Tuesday
Date ..../......./.......

Description	Amount
Total	

Wednesday
Date ..../......./.......

Description	Amount
Total	

Thursday
Date ..../......./.......

Description	Amount
Total	

Weekly Expense Tracker

Total Expenses :

Balance :

Friday
Date ....../....../......

Description	Amount
Total	

Saturday
Date ....../....../......

Description	Amount
Total	

Sunday
Date ....../....../......

Description	Amount
Total	

Notes

Weekly Expense Tracker

Month : _____   **Week Of :** _____   **Budget :** _____

Monday   Date ..../......./.......

Description	Amount
Total	

Tuesday   Date ..../......./.......

Description	Amount
Total	

Wednesday   Date ..../......./.......

Description	Amount
Total	

Thursday   Date ..../......./.......

Description	Amount
Total	

Weekly Expense Tracker

Total Expenses :   **Balance :**

Friday   Date ..../......./.......

Description	Amount
Total	

Saturday   Date ..../......./.......

Description	Amount
Total	

Sunday   Date ..../......./.......

Description	Amount
Total	

Notes

Weekly Expense Tracker

Month : _____   **Week Of :** _____   **Budget :** _____

Monday   Date ..../......../........

Description	Amount
Total	

Tuesday   Date ..../......../........

Description	Amount
Total	

Wednesday   Date ..../......../........

Description	Amount
Total	

Thursday   Date ..../......../........

Description	Amount
Total	

Weekly Expense Tracker

Total Expenses :

Balance :

Friday

Date ..../......./.......

Description	Amount
Total	

Saturday

Date ..../......./.......

Description	Amount
Total	

Sunday

Date ..../......./.......

Description	Amount
Total	

Notes

_____
_____
_____
_____
_____
_____
_____
_____
_____
_____

Weekly Expense Tracker

Month : _____   Week Of : _____   Budget : _____

Monday Date ....../....../......

Description	Amount
Total	

Tuesday Date ....../....../......

Description	Amount
Total	

Wednesday Date ....../....../......

Description	Amount
Total	

Thursday Date ....../....../......

Description	Amount
Total	

Weekly Expense Tracker

Total Expenses : **Balance :**

Friday

Date …..../…...../…......

Description	Amount
Total	

Saturday

Date …..../…...../…......

Description	Amount
Total	

Sunday

Date …..../…...../…......

Description	Amount
Total	

Notes

Weekly Expense Tracker

Month : _____   Week Of : _____   Budget : _____

Monday   Date ..../......./.......

Description	Amount
Total	

Tuesday   Date ..../......./.......

Description	Amount
Total	

Wednesday   Date ..../......./.......

Description	Amount
Total	

Thursday   Date ..../......./.......

Description	Amount
Total	

Weekly Expense Tracker

Total Expenses :

Balance :

Friday

Date ..../......./.......

Description	Amount
Total	

Saturday

Date ..../......./.......

Description	Amount
Total	

Sunday

Date ..../......./.......

Description	Amount
Total	

Notes

Monthly Budget

Expenses

Income		
Income 1		
Income 2		
Other Income		
TOTAL INCOME		

Month :

Budget :

Bill To Be Paid	Date Due	Amount	Paid	Note
			◯	
			◯	
			◯	
			◯	
			◯	
			◯	
			◯	
			◯	
			◯	
			◯	
			◯	
			◯	
			◯	
			◯	
			◯	
			◯	
			◯	
			◯	
			◯	
TOTAL				

Monthly Budget

Other Expenses	Date	Amount	Note
TOTAL			

TOTAL INCOME

TOTAL EXPENSES

DIFFERENCE

Notes

Weekly Expense Tracker

Month :   **Week Of :**   **Budget :**

Monday   Date ....../....../......

Description	Amount
Total	

Tuesday   Date ....../....../......

Description	Amount
Total	

Wednesday   Date ....../....../......

Description	Amount
Total	

Thursday   Date ....../....../......

Description	Amount
Total	

Weekly Expense Tracker

Total Expenses :

Balance :

Friday
Date ..../......./.......

Description	Amount
Total	

Saturday
Date ..../......./.......

Description	Amount
Total	

Sunday
Date ..../......./.......

Description	Amount
Total	

Notes

Weekly Expense Tracker

Month : _____   **Week Of :** _____   **Budget :** _____

Monday   Date ..../......./.......

Description	Amount
Total	

Tuesday   Date ..../......./.......

Description	Amount
Total	

Wednesday   Date ..../......./.......

Description	Amount
Total	

Thursday   Date ..../......./.......

Description	Amount
Total	

Weekly Expense Tracker

Total Expenses :   **Balance :**

Friday   Date ..../......./.......

Description	Amount
Total	

Saturday   Date ..../......./.......

Description	Amount
Total	

Sunday   Date ..../......./.......

Description	Amount
Total	

Notes

Weekly Expense Tracker

Month :   **Week Of :**   **Budget :**

Monday   Date ..../......./.......

Description	Amount
Total	

Tuesday   Date ..../......./.......

Description	Amount
Total	

Wednesday   Date ..../......./.......

Description	Amount
Total	

Thursday   Date ..../......./.......

Description	Amount
Total	

Weekly Expense Tracker

Total Expenses :   **Balance :**

Friday

Date ..../......./.......

Description	Amount
Total	

Saturday

Date ..../......./.......

Description	Amount
Total	

Sunday

Date ..../......./.......

Description	Amount
Total	

Notes

Weekly Expense Tracker

Month : _____   Week Of : _____   Budget : _____

Monday   Date ..../......./.......

Description	Amount
Total	

Tuesday   Date ..../......./.......

Description	Amount
Total	

Wednesday   Date ..../......./.......

Description	Amount
Total	

Thursday   Date ..../......./.......

Description	Amount
Total	

Weekly Expense Tracker

Total Expenses :   **Balance :**

Friday   Date ..../......./.......

Description	Amount
Total	

Saturday   Date ..../......./.......

Description	Amount
Total	

Sunday   Date ..../......./.......

Description	Amount
Total	

Notes

Weekly Expense Tracker

Month :   **Week Of :**   **Budget :**

Monday   Date ....../....../......

Description	Amount
Total	

Tuesday   Date ....../....../......

Description	Amount
Total	

Wednesday   Date ....../....../......

Description	Amount
Total	

Thursday   Date ....../....../......

Description	Amount
Total	

Weekly Expense Tracker

Total Expenses :   **Balance :**

Friday   Date ..../......./.......

Description	Amount
Total	

Saturday   Date ..../......./.......

Description	Amount
Total	

Sunday   Date ..../......./.......

Description	Amount
Total	

Notes

Monthly Budget

Income		
Income 1		
Income 2		
Other Income		
TOTAL INCOME		

Expenses

Month :

Budget :

Bill To Be Paid	Date Due	Amount	Paid	Note
			◯	
			◯	
			◯	
			◯	
			◯	
			◯	
			◯	
			◯	
			◯	
			◯	
			◯	
			◯	
			◯	
			◯	
			◯	
			◯	
			◯	
			◯	
			◯	
TOTAL				

Monthly Budget

Other Expenses	Date	Amount	Note
TOTAL			

		Notes
TOTAL INCOME		
TOTAL EXPENSES		
DIFFERENCE		

Weekly Expense Tracker

Month :   **Week Of :**   **Budget :**

Monday   Date ..../......./.......

Description	Amount
Total	

Tuesday   Date ..../......./.......

Description	Amount
Total	

Wednesday   Date ..../......./.......

Description	Amount
Total	

Thursday   Date ..../......./.......

Description	Amount
Total	

Weekly Expense Tracker

Total Expenses :   **Balance :**

Friday   Date ..../......./.......

Description	Amount
Total	

Saturday   Date ..../......./.......

Description	Amount
Total	

Sunday   Date ..../......./.......

Description	Amount
Total	

Notes

_____

_____

_____

_____

_____

_____

_____

_____

_____

_____

_____

Weekly Expense Tracker

Month : _____   **Week Of :** _____   **Budget :** _____

Monday   Date ……/……/……

Description	Amount
Total	

Tuesday   Date ……/……/……

Description	Amount
Total	

Wednesday   Date ……/……/……

Description	Amount
Total	

Thursday   Date ……/……/……

Description	Amount
Total	

Weekly Expense Tracker

Total Expenses : **Balance :**

Friday
Date ..../......./.......

Description	Amount
Total	

Saturday
Date ..../......./.......

Description	Amount
Total	

Sunday
Date ..../......./.......

Description	Amount
Total	

Notes

_____
_____
_____
_____
_____
_____
_____
_____
_____

Weekly Expense Tracker

Month : _____   Week Of : _____   Budget : _____

Monday   Date ..../......./.......

Description	Amount
Total	

Tuesday   Date ..../......./.......

Description	Amount
Total	

Wednesday   Date ..../......./.......

Description	Amount
Total	

Thursday   Date ..../......./.......

Description	Amount
Total	

Weekly Expense Tracker

Total Expenses : _____   **Balance :** _____

Friday
Date ....../....../......

Description	Amount
Total	

Saturday
Date ....../....../......

Description	Amount
Total	

Sunday
Date ....../....../......

Description	Amount
Total	

Notes
_____
_____
_____
_____
_____
_____
_____
_____
_____
_____

Weekly Expense Tracker

Month : _____   Week Of : _____   Budget : _____

Monday
Date ....../....../......

Description	Amount
Total	

Tuesday
Date ....../....../......

Description	Amount
Total	

Wednesday
Date ....../....../......

Description	Amount
Total	

Thursday
Date ....../....../......

Description	Amount
Total	

Weekly Expense Tracker

Total Expenses :   **Balance :**

Friday

Date ..../......./.......

Description	Amount
Total	

Saturday

Date ..../......./.......

Description	Amount
Total	

Sunday

Date ..../......./.......

Description	Amount
Total	

Notes

_____

_____

_____

_____

_____

_____

_____

_____

_____

Weekly Expense Tracker

Month : _____   Week Of : _____   Budget : _____

Monday

Date ..../......../........

Description	Amount
Total	

Tuesday

Date ..../......../........

Description	Amount
Total	

Wednesday

Date ..../......../........

Description	Amount
Total	

Thursday

Date ..../......../........

Description	Amount
Total	

Weekly Expense Tracker

Total Expenses : _____   **Balance :** _____

Friday   Date ..../......./.......

Description	Amount
Total	

Saturday   Date ..../......./.......

Description	Amount
Total	

Sunday   Date ..../......./.......

Description	Amount
Total	

Notes

_____

_____

_____

_____

_____

_____

_____

_____

_____

_____

Monthly Budget

Income	
Income 1	
Income 2	
Other Income	
TOTAL INCOME	

Expenses

Month :

Budget :

Bill To Be Paid	Date Due	Amount	Paid	Note
			◯	
			◯	
			◯	
			◯	
			◯	
			◯	
			◯	
			◯	
			◯	
			◯	
			◯	
			◯	
			◯	
			◯	
			◯	
			◯	
			◯	
			◯	
TOTAL				

Monthly Budget

Other Expenses	Date	Amount	Note
TOTAL			

TOTAL INCOME

TOTAL EXPENSES

DIFFERENCE

Notes

_____

_____

_____

_____

_____

Weekly Expense Tracker

Month :

Week Of :

Budget :

Monday
Date ....../....../......

Description	Amount
Total	

Tuesday
Date ....../....../......

Description	Amount
Total	

Wednesday
Date ....../....../......

Description	Amount
Total	

Thursday
Date ....../....../......

Description	Amount
Total	

Weekly Expense Tracker

Total Expenses :   **Balance :**

Friday   Date ....../....../......

Description	Amount
Total	

Saturday   Date ....../....../......

Description	Amount
Total	

Sunday   Date ....../....../......

Description	Amount
Total	

Notes

_____

_____

_____

_____

_____

_____

_____

_____

_____

_____

Weekly Expense Tracker

Month : _____   Week Of : _____   Budget : _____

Monday   Date ..../......./.......

Description	Amount
Total	

Tuesday   Date ..../......./.......

Description	Amount
Total	

Wednesday   Date ..../......./.......

Description	Amount
Total	

Thursday   Date ..../......./.......

Description	Amount
Total	

Weekly Expense Tracker

Total Expenses :   **Balance :**

Friday   Date ..../....../.......

Description	Amount
Total	

Saturday   Date ..../....../.......

Description	Amount
Total	

Sunday   Date ..../....../.......

Description	Amount
Total	

Notes

_____

_____

_____

_____

_____

_____

_____

_____

_____

Weekly Expense Tracker

Month : _____   **Week Of :** _____   **Budget :** _____

Monday

Date ..../......./.......

Description	Amount
Total	

Tuesday

Date ..../......./.......

Description	Amount
Total	

Wednesday

Date ..../......./.......

Description	Amount
Total	

Thursday

Date ..../......./.......

Description	Amount
Total	

Weekly Expense Tracker

Total Expenses :   **Balance :**

Friday   Date ..../......./.......

Description	Amount
Total	

Saturday   Date ..../......./.......

Description	Amount
Total	

Sunday   Date ..../......./.......

Description	Amount
Total	

Notes

Weekly Expense Tracker

Month : _____   Week Of : _____   Budget : _____

Monday   Date ..../......./.......

Description	Amount
Total	

Tuesday   Date ..../......./.......

Description	Amount
Total	

Wednesday   Date ..../......./.......

Description	Amount
Total	

Thursday   Date ..../......./.......

Description	Amount
Total	

Weekly Expense Tracker

Total Expenses :　　　　　　　　　　　　　　**Balance :**

Friday　　　Date ..../......./.......

Description	Amount
Total	

Saturday　　　Date ..../......./.......

Description	Amount
Total	

Sunday　　　Date ..../......./.......

Description	Amount
Total	

Notes

Weekly Expense Tracker

Month : _____   **Week Of :** _____   **Budget :** _____

Monday   Date ..../......./.......

Description	Amount
Total	

Tuesday   Date ..../......./.......

Description	Amount
Total	

Wednesday   Date ..../......./.......

Description	Amount
Total	

Thursday   Date ..../......./.......

Description	Amount
Total	

Weekly Expense Tracker

Total Expenses :   **Balance :**

Friday

Date ..../......./.......

Description	Amount
Total	

Saturday

Date ..../......./.......

Description	Amount
Total	

Sunday

Date ..../......./.......

Description	Amount
Total	

Notes

Monthly Budget

Expenses

Income	
Income 1	
Income 2	
Other Income	
TOTAL INCOME	

Month :

Budget :

Bill To Be Paid	Date Due	Amount	Paid	Note
			○	
			○	
			○	
			○	
			○	
			○	
			○	
			○	
			○	
			○	
			○	
			○	
			○	
			○	
			○	
			○	
			○	
			○	
			○	
TOTAL				

Monthly Budget

Other Expenses	Date	Amount	Note
TOTAL			

TOTAL INCOME

TOTAL EXPENSES

DIFFERENCE

Notes

Weekly Expense Tracker

Month : _____   Week Of : _____   Budget : _____

Monday   Date ..../......./.......

Description	Amount
Total	

Tuesday   Date ..../......./.......

Description	Amount
Total	

Wednesday   Date ..../......./.......

Description	Amount
Total	

Thursday   Date ..../......./.......

Description	Amount
Total	

Weekly Expense Tracker

Total Expenses :

Balance :

Friday
Date ..../......./.......

Description	Amount
Total	

Saturday
Date ..../......./.......

Description	Amount
Total	

Sunday
Date ..../......./.......

Description	Amount
Total	

Notes

Weekly Expense Tracker

Month : _____   Week Of : _____   Budget : _____

Monday   Date ..../......./.......

Description	Amount
Total	

Tuesday   Date ..../......./.......

Description	Amount
Total	

Wednesday   Date ..../......./.......

Description	Amount
Total	

Thursday   Date ..../......./.......

Description	Amount
Total	

Weekly Expense Tracker

Total Expenses :   **Balance :**

Friday   Date ..../......./.......

Description	Amount
Total	

Saturday   Date ..../......./.......

Description	Amount
Total	

Sunday   Date ..../......./.......

Description	Amount
Total	

Notes

_____

_____

_____

_____

_____

_____

_____

_____

_____

_____

_____

Weekly Expense Tracker

Month : _____   **Week Of :** _____   **Budget :** _____

Monday   Date ..../......./.......

Description	Amount
Total	

Tuesday   Date ..../......./.......

Description	Amount
Total	

Wednesday   Date ..../......./.......

Description	Amount
Total	

Thursday   Date ..../......./.......

Description	Amount
Total	

Weekly Expense Tracker

Total Expenses :   **Balance :**

Friday   Date ....../....../......

Description	Amount
Total	

Saturday   Date ....../....../......

Description	Amount
Total	

Sunday   Date ....../....../......

Description	Amount
Total	

Notes

Weekly Expense Tracker

Month : _____ **Week Of :** _____ **Budget :** _____

Monday Date ..../......./.......

Description	Amount
Total	

Tuesday Date ..../......./.......

Description	Amount
Total	

Wednesday Date ..../......./.......

Description	Amount
Total	

Thursday Date ..../......./.......

Description	Amount
Total	

Weekly Expense Tracker

Total Expenses :　　　　　　　　　　　　　**Balance :**

Friday　　　　Date ..../......./.......

Description	Amount
Total	

Saturday　　　　Date ..../......./.......

Description	Amount
Total	

Sunday　　　　Date ..../......./.......

Description	Amount
Total	

Notes

Weekly Expense Tracker

Month :　　　　　　　　　　**Week Of :**　　　　　　　　**Budget :**

Monday　　Date ..../......./.......

Description	Amount
Total	

Tuesday　　Date ..../......./.......

Description	Amount
Total	

Wednesday　　Date ..../......./.......

Description	Amount
Total	

Thursday　　Date ..../......./.......

Description	Amount
Total	

Weekly Expense Tracker

Total Expenses :

Balance :

Friday

Date …..../…..../…....

Description	Amount
Total	

Saturday

Date …..../…..../…....

Description	Amount
Total	

Sunday

Date …..../…..../…....

Description	Amount
Total	

Notes

Monthly Budget

Expenses

Income		
Income 1		
Income 2		
Other Income		
TOTAL INCOME		

Month :

Budget :

Bill To Be Paid	Date Due	Amount	Paid	Note
			◯	
			◯	
			◯	
			◯	
			◯	
			◯	
			◯	
			◯	
			◯	
			◯	
			◯	
			◯	
			◯	
			◯	
			◯	
			◯	
			◯	
			◯	
			◯	
TOTAL				

Monthly Budget

Other Expenses	Date	Amount	Note
TOTAL			

TOTAL INCOME

TOTAL EXPENSES

DIFFERENCE

Notes

Weekly Expense Tracker

Month :   **Week Of :**   **Budget :**

Monday   Date ..../......./.......

Description	Amount
Total	

Tuesday   Date ..../......./.......

Description	Amount
Total	

Wednesday   Date ..../......./.......

Description	Amount
Total	

Thursday   Date ..../......./.......

Description	Amount
Total	

Weekly Expense Tracker

Total Expenses : **Balance :**

Friday
Date ..../......./.......

Description	Amount
Total	

Saturday
Date ..../......./.......

Description	Amount
Total	

Sunday
Date ..../......./.......

Description	Amount
Total	

Notes

Weekly Expense Tracker

Month : **Week Of :** **Budget :**

Monday   Date ..../......./.......

Description	Amount
Total	

Tuesday   Date ..../......./.......

Description	Amount
Total	

Wednesday   Date ..../......./.......

Description	Amount
Total	

Thursday   Date ..../......./.......

Description	Amount
Total	

Weekly Expense Tracker

Total Expenses :

Balance :

Friday

Date ..../......./.......

Description	Amount
Total	

Saturday

Date ..../......./.......

Description	Amount
Total	

Sunday

Date ..../......./.......

Description	Amount
Total	

Notes

Weekly Expense Tracker

Month :   **Week Of :**   **Budget :**

Monday   Date ..../......./.......

Description	Amount
Total	

Tuesday   Date ..../......./.......

Description	Amount
Total	

Wednesday   Date ..../......./.......

Description	Amount
Total	

Thursday   Date ..../......./.......

Description	Amount
Total	

Weekly Expense Tracker

Total Expenses :   **Balance :**

Friday   Date ....../....../......

Description	Amount
Total	

Saturday   Date ....../....../......

Description	Amount
Total	

Sunday   Date ....../....../......

Description	Amount
Total	

Notes

_____

_____

_____

_____

_____

_____

_____

_____

_____

Weekly Expense Tracker

Month : _____ Week Of : _____ Budget : _____

Monday
Date ..../......./.......

Description	Amount
Total	

Tuesday
Date ..../......./.......

Description	Amount
Total	

Wednesday
Date ..../......./.......

Description	Amount
Total	

Thursday
Date ..../......./.......

Description	Amount
Total	

Weekly Expense Tracker

Total Expenses :   **Balance :**

Friday
Date ....../....../......

Description	Amount
Total	

Saturday
Date ....../....../......

Description	Amount
Total	

Sunday
Date ....../....../......

Description	Amount
Total	

Notes

Weekly Expense Tracker

Month : _____   **Week Of :** _____   **Budget :** _____

Monday   Date ..../......./.......

Description	Amount
Total	

Tuesday   Date ..../......./.......

Description	Amount
Total	

Wednesday   Date ..../......./.......

Description	Amount
Total	

Thursday   Date ..../......./.......

Description	Amount
Total	

Weekly Expense Tracker

Total Expenses :   **Balance :**

Friday   Date ..../......./.......

Description	Amount
Total	

Saturday   Date ..../......./.......

Description	Amount
Total	

Sunday   Date ..../......./.......

Description	Amount
Total	

Notes

Monthly Budget

Income		
Income 1		
Income 2		
Other Income		
TOTAL INCOME		

Expenses

Month :

Budget :

Bill To Be Paid	Date Due	Amount	Paid	Note
			◯	
			◯	
			◯	
			◯	
			◯	
			◯	
			◯	
			◯	
			◯	
			◯	
			◯	
			◯	
			◯	
			◯	
			◯	
			◯	
			◯	
			◯	
			◯	
TOTAL				

Monthly Budget

Other Expenses	Date	Amount	Note
TOTAL			

TOTAL INCOME

TOTAL EXPENSES

DIFFERENCE

Notes

Weekly Expense Tracker

Month : _____   Week Of : _____   Budget : _____

Monday
Date ..../......../........

Description	Amount
Total	

Tuesday
Date ..../......../........

Description	Amount
Total	

Wednesday
Date ..../......../........

Description	Amount
Total	

Thursday
Date ..../......../........

Description	Amount
Total	

Weekly Expense Tracker

Total Expenses : _____

Balance : _____

Friday

Date ..../......./.......

Description	Amount
Total	

Saturday

Date ..../......./.......

Description	Amount
Total	

Sunday

Date ..../......./.......

Description	Amount
Total	

Notes

_____

_____

_____

_____

_____

_____

_____

_____

_____

_____

Weekly Expense Tracker

Month : _____   Week Of : _____   Budget : _____

Monday
Date ..../......./.......

Description	Amount
Total	

Tuesday
Date ..../......./.......

Description	Amount
Total	

Wednesday
Date ..../......./.......

Description	Amount
Total	

Thursday
Date ..../......./.......

Description	Amount
Total	

Weekly Expense Tracker

Total Expenses :

Balance :

Friday
Date ..../......./.......

Description	Amount
Total	

Saturday
Date ..../......./.......

Description	Amount
Total	

Sunday
Date ..../......./.......

Description	Amount
Total	

Notes

Weekly Expense Tracker

Month : _____   Week Of : _____   Budget : _____

Monday   Date ..../......./.......

Description	Amount
Total	

Tuesday   Date ..../......./.......

Description	Amount
Total	

Wednesday   Date ..../......./.......

Description	Amount
Total	

Thursday   Date ..../......./.......

Description	Amount
Total	

Weekly Expense Tracker

Total Expenses :   **Balance :**

Friday   Date ....../....../......

Description	Amount
Total	

Saturday   Date ....../....../......

Description	Amount
Total	

Sunday   Date ....../....../......

Description	Amount
Total	

Notes

_____

_____

_____

_____

_____

_____

_____

_____

_____

_____

_____

Weekly Expense Tracker

Month : _____   Week Of : _____   Budget : _____

Monday
Date ..../......./.......

Description	Amount
Total	

Tuesday
Date ..../......./.......

Description	Amount
Total	

Wednesday
Date ..../......./.......

Description	Amount
Total	

Thursday
Date ..../......./.......

Description	Amount
Total	

Weekly Expense Tracker

Total Expenses :

Balance :

Friday
Date ..../......./.......

Description	Amount
Total	

Saturday
Date ..../......./.......

Description	Amount
Total	

Sunday
Date ..../......./.......

Description	Amount
Total	

Notes

Weekly Expense Tracker

Month : _____   Week Of : _____   Budget : _____

Monday   Date ....../....../......

Description	Amount
Total	

Tuesday   Date ....../....../......

Description	Amount
Total	

Wednesday   Date ....../....../......

Description	Amount
Total	

Thursday   Date ....../....../......

Description	Amount
Total	

Weekly Expense Tracker

Total Expenses :

Balance :

Friday

Date ..../......./.......

Description	Amount
Total	

Saturday

Date ..../......./.......

Description	Amount
Total	

Sunday

Date ..../......./.......

Description	Amount
Total	

Notes

Notes

Made in United States
Orlando, FL
13 July 2022

19718042R00083